THE
WORLD
CUP
-of-
SOUPS

A RECIPE BOOK
Chef Mark Alan Scott

To order additional copies of this book, contact:
Xlibris LLC
1-888-795-4274
www.Xlibris.com
Orders@Xlibris.com

DEDICATION

This book is dedicated to all the hard working and industrious people who plug away day after day,
night after night cutting themselves and burning themselves to cook for other people.

Thanks to all the great co - workers, that through diligence and hard work have made my job a heck of alot easier.
A heartfelt thanks.

THE WORLD CUP OF SOUPS:

The premise of this book was to celebrate the Greatest sporting event in the world. The World Cup of Football, or as us North Americans know as soccer. This incredible sporting event takes place every 4 years and takes over 3 years to find out what teams remain at the end. After years of vying for The World Cup, only 32 teams remain. The original concept was to do a cookbook of soups, strictly from the teams that qualified, so there will be 32 recipes in the book, but that would make for an extremely short book so I have included information about making stocks in order to make the soups as good as possible, also making cream soups with alternate ways to thicken without using flour, the use of fresh herbs as compared to dry herbs. Etc Etc...Oh also of note, I realized that all these soups are of the cooked nature, not a single cold soup. So I decided that to celebrate the special run by the brilliant Spanish National Team that has won two European championships and the last World Cup, It is only fitting that the one and only cold soup in the entire book should be the absolutely brilliant Soup from Andalusia - Gazpacho. A fabulous soup to commemorate a fabulous soccer team.

SPAIN  RANKED # 1

Gazpacho Andaluz

INGREDIENTS: Chop all the ingredients except the parsley and cilantro. Add those at the end as a garnish.

- 4 ripe juicy tomatoes
- 1 cucumber-peeled and seeds and skin removed
- ½ red bell pepper
- ½ red onion-small dice
- 1 cloves garlic
- ¼ of a bunch of parsley-chopped fine-(add at the end after everything is pureed)
- a bit of chopped cilantro-chopped fine-(add at the end after everything is pureed)
- 1 cup of vegetable stock-optional
- 3 oz/100 ml red wine vinegar
- 3 oz/100 ml olive oil
- 1 oz/56 grams of bread crumbs
- Salt and pepper, thyme and a few chillies.

The method for this soup is place all the ingredients in a bowl except the parsley, cilantro and bread crumbs as well as the vinegar. Puree all the vegetables and then add the parsley, cilantro both chopped by hand and the bread crumbs. Season to taste with salt pepper and the olive oil and chillies. Add the red wine vinegar at the end, the amount you want to taste. The vegetable stock is only if you want the soup a little thinner.

Please note that all these recipes are based on traditional recipes, and any changes in the recipes are my doing and nobody elses. I have tried to make the recipes as easy as possible, and to try to give as much information as possible without getting too technical.

I always tell my darling wife to put as much passion, respect and love into anything you do...and this includes cooking. So enjoy this book, enjoy making the soups and enjoy having friends over to watch the World Cup, eat some soups that you have made, have a glass of wine and watch the greatest game in the world.

All of these soups can be prepared or prepped ahead of time so as to make the cooking time shorter and simpler to do. Like cutting your vegetables ahead of time, making your stock ahead of time, cooking beans the day before and so on and so forth so as to save time.

 Unfortunately I started this piece of work around October of 2013, and between running a kitchen at a 220 seat sports bar and trying to keep some semblance of a normal life, I constantly found the World Cup rankings changing every time a national team played. I tried to draw the line somewhere or I would be working on this book until it was too late to try to get this published. It's still no guarantee. So with all the changes since I first started this, I have probably made over 70 different soups.

I am revising this book for the umpteenth time and now that 32 teams have now qualified I can now carry on with other aspects of the book. My tough luck though - as two of my favourite soups are no longer in the top 60 rankings. One of my favorite soup was the Gumbo from Haiti and the Irish Guinness Onion Soup with mature Irish cheese croutons. They were both superb. Oh Well.

On a dour note, I had photos taken for all the soups, but I found out just recently that the photos were S*****y and couldn't be used. My humblest apologies for this mix up. I guess I am more accomplished making soups rather than taking photographs. I will try to include photos of soups on game day, on the proposed web site.

SEASONINGS AND SPICES:

Throughout the book you will notice that I use homemade stocks and lots of vegetables, garlic and herbs, cracked pepper and as a last resort salt. With a good stock, herbs and spices one can get the desired effect or taste while watching your salt intake. When working with fresh herbs, you add them near the completion of the soup. When working with dried herbs one adds them while the soup is cooking. With fresh herbs you have what is called a volatile oil, that when added to something, the flavour is instantly incorporated into what you are cooking. With dry herbs the flavour needs to cook in for a longer period of time.

THANK YOUS & ACKNOWLEDGEMENTS:

Boy do I have a lot of thank yous, to a lot of people whom without their support this would not be happening. If I missed some names and references along the way, please forgive me my errors and omissions. It all boils down to the mere fact I want this book to be longer than the Thank Yous. So here goes…

Thanks to my darling wife Kathy - for putting up with me and my crazy hours that I have worked over the years as a chef. Well just for putting up with me period, and of course thank you for the title.

To my wonderful children - Dakota who convinced me to try to do this book. To my son Nicholas Tchir for all the work that he has to do, and for the work he has already done - The cover art, the computer expertise etc.. and done all on promises. To Caitlin for her encouragement and for being one of the official taste testers, and for her outstanding wit and unique sense of humour.

To Glenn Jensen and Jenny Yates - for their unwavering support and for allowing me to use their establishment to show off these soups over the years and to the regulars at my place of work who have encouraged me to do this.

To Everett -who constantly threatens me with grievous bodily harm if I do not complete this project, and to his wife Kathy who is always able to restrain him and for their help with the financial wherewithal to do this. My sincerest thanks.

Near last but not least: a special dedication to two of the most unique and special people I have had the luck and fortune to know - to Chris and Gwen for their undying and unwavering friendship.

And a very special Thank you to Mr.Peter Warring - (Rest in peace) - For having had the honour of his friendship. I am blessed to have had him in my corner since the late 1970's until he passed away a few years back.

Thanks to Jeff, for your support and friendship. You have always been there.

And a last Thank you, and this is a special Thank you - thanks to the BEAUTIFUL GAME of Football /Soccer and the players that have graced the pitch. Maybe one day I will tell what kind of influence the World Cup has had with me over the years.

NOTES ON POTATOES:

I am not sure as to why I'm doing a few notes on potatoes, but not all potatoes are created equal..Some potatoes have a higher starch content, some have a higher sugar content, and some are just perfect for certain soups. In Canada we have Russets, Kennenbecs, Yukon Gold, etc.. the potato of choice in this book is the tried and true Russet. But you can use what is available to you. If you are going to thicken a soup using potatoes, then use the one with a high starch content.

COOKING WITH OILS-USING BUTTER:

There has been a lot of information available lately about the changes and health issues about heating oils, meaning some oils should be used cold and not heated. Heating oils creates a molecular change in the oil which is believed to create carcinogens. So some oils are more suited for cooking than others. Most people in Canada use Canola oil,otherwise known as rapeseed.There has been a huge movement on the benefits of cooking with Coconut oil which I understand handles heat extremely well and is safer for you to use, but the taste of your soup can be slightly altered because the oil tastes like Coconut. But do remember that you are only using the oil to saute your vegetable for making the soup. If you are using a traditional recipe for a cream soup I use good old butter. If you want to do serious sauteing one can use Ghee which is clarified butter, with all the milk solids removed so you have what is called well-clarified butter. This handles the heat better without burning.

NOTE AND REVISIONS FOR MAKING CREAM SOUPS WITHOUT USING FLOUR:

For those of you who shy away from flour for either health reasons or other reasons you can still make a cream soup without using flour.Traditional cream soups are usually made with butter and adding flour - hence making what is called a Roux. To change the method for making a cream soup bypassing the use of flour, just saute your vegetables with a little bit of oil or butter and carry on with the making of your soup. When the time comes to thicken the soup add a slurry of cornstarch and cold water to the soup until you get the desired thickness and finish with a bit of heavy cream or whipping cream to give the soup the final touch or smoothness you want. It is really quite easy using this method. If you don't have cornstarch use sago sago or rice starch.

NOTE ON SEASONINGS:

Hopefully you will have noticed that throughout this book I am constantly mentioning seasoning your soup. Over the years I have made a concerted effort to use as little salt as possible, using herbs and spices instead.This will take a bit of effort as we have become so used to salt that when cooking not just soups but all foods we tend to find foods tasting bland unless we add salt.

This can be fixed again by using fresh cracked peppercorns or fresh herbs / dry herbs, hot sauces etc...Adding salt only as a last measure and only after seasoning your soup with spices and herbs. But the real key to a flavourful soup is a good stock. So this is what I am going to get into next.

STOCKS:

A good soup starts with a good stock, this book is built around this practice. You don't have to be a chef to make a good stock. Depending on the types of soups you are making, certain stocks take longer to make and are a little more involved, but they are not difficult to do. Always save your vegetable trimmings, carrot skins, celery scraps and greens, onion skins and a bay leaf, and whole peppercorns and cold water. If you are going to make an Oxtail soup (England) you would roast the oxtails and vegetable trimmings to get that beautiful rich flavour.Then add cold water, peppercorns,bay leaf, etc and slowly simmer your stock for about an hour and a half. Key word being Simmer. You do not want to boil a stock hard as the fat from meats and chickens will meld with the stock and you will have a cloudy and fatty stock which you just don't want. The cooking time for stocks varies depending on what type of stock you are making. Beef or veal stocks take the longest, chicken stock a little less than beef / veal, with vegetable or fish stocks taking the shortest amount of time. Roasting certainly adds to the colour and depth of your stock, but I don't usually roast chicken for stock. Potato stocks are also a great addition to soups. Throughout the book you will see recipes that have potatoes in them, that is why I save the stock when cooking potatoes.So to get to the main point - cook beef and veal stocks for about 2 hours, Chicken stock for about 1 hour and a bit and vegetable or fish stock for just short of an hour. Careful with fish stock as it can cloud quite easily. So when you make a fish stock simmer for about 45 minutes and let sit - all the blood that was in the bones will settle on the bottom when cooling. Always strain your stocks.

NOTE FOR VEGETARIANS:

This is quite a simple alternative for all these soups in the book, if you want a vegetarian soups just omit the meats or fish. Very straight forward. Just make sure you compensate for your lack of animal product with lots of vegetables and stuff. But keep in mind that some soups should be kept just the way they are meant to be.

NOTE ON FRESH HERBS:

Remember that in certain areas around the world fresh herbs are in short supply and very seasonal.Thanks to the advent of greenhouses etc, fresh herbs are more readily available. Using fresh herbs simply make the soups far more tasty and flavourful no doubt, but if you don't have fresh herbs use dry herbs instead. The procedure for using dry herbs as compared to fresh is you add dry herbs sooner during the cooking procedure than you would with fresh. Fresh herbs you add near the end when you are going to finish seasoning the soup, as the volatile oils in the fresh herbs are far more pronounced and should not be wasted or lost by adding to soon.

A SHORT NOTE ON USING FLOUR:

When I use flour in a soup, the flour most suitable is an unbleached white flour. If you have an intolerance to gluten or simply do not want to use white flour, you can use Amaranth or Millet which is Celiac friendly for those not wanting to use regular flour. Rice flour, almond flour and coconut flour are alternatives,especially with people with a gluten intolerance. These flours are a bit more finicky and they will alter the flavour of the soup and the thickening capabilities are different as well. Plus they may be expensive to get. CornStarch, Arrowroot, Tapioca and Sorghum are all Celiac friendly as well, but make sure that The cornstarch is labeled Gluten free, as some cornstarch can be contaminated in processing.

TABLE OF CONTENTS

Group A – Page 13

Group B – Page 19

Group C – Page 25

Group D – Page 31

Group E – Page 37

Group F – Page 43

Group G – Page 49

Group H – Page 57

A GLOSSARY OF TERMS AND A FEW TIPS

You will come across terms or words that may not mean much to you, so I will mention the words with simple explanations to their meanings. After 40 years in the restaurant business I tend to not even think about what the terms mean. Also included are little tips to make the process of making soups simpler.

#1 - Chiffonade : Refers to thin sliced herbs or greens, rolled and shaved thin.

#2 - Slurry : This is a mixture of cornstarch and cold water / flour and cold water - is a quick easy way to thicken something.

#3 - Zeste : This is the skin of a citrus fruit - lemon, lime etc. Use a zester, if you don't have one, use a peeler and then chop the skin really small. Add according to taste.

#4 - Dollop : Refers to a spoon full of something - usually a garnish. Like a dollop of sour cream.

#5 - Ooomph - Just a little something from me - meaning a little pizzazz, a little kick etc.. add some spice. Etc

#6 - Oh yes, one of the most important things to know - Place a wet cloth under your cutting board. This prevents the cutting board from moving about when using it, this will prevent you cutting yourself.

#7 - That's probably enough for now.

The Groups of Teams that have Qualified for 2014 World Cup. 32 teams in total. 8 groups of 4

Group - A   Brazil # 10 - Black bean and Chicken soup

Croatia # 16 - Northern Croatian Black Bean soup

Mexico # 21 - Albondigas soup

Cameroon # 50 - Groundnut (Peanut) and Chicken soup

Group - B   Spain # 1 - Caldo Gallego

Netherlands # 9 - Dutch Potato and Bacon soup

Chile # 15 - Spicy Seafood soup

Australia # 56 - Australian Pumpkin soup

Group - C	Colombia # 4 - Chicken and Potato soup
	Greece # 12 - Mavromatika Fasolia me Loukanko
	Cote d'Ivoire # 17 - Yam and Chicken soup
	Japan #48- Red Miso and Pork soup
Group - D	Uruguay # 6 - Chupin de Pescado soup
	Italy # 7 - A Wedding soup
	England # 13 - Oxtail soup
	Costa Rica # 32 - Black Bean and Pork soup
Group - E	Switzerland # 8 - Potato and Bacon soup
	France # 20 - Pumpkin, Black Bean and Ham soup
	Ecuador # 23 - Summer Squash soup
	Honduras # 43 - Sopa de Caracol soup
Group - F	Argentina # 3 - Locro de Argentine / Navy Bean and Corn soup
	Bosnia and Herzegovina # 19 - Chicken, Bacon and Okra soup
	Iran # 34 - Asheh Reshteh soup
	Nigeria # 41 - Okra, Chicken and Uziza Leaf soup
Group - G	Germany # 2 - Graupensuppe / German Barley soup
	Portugal # 5 - Kahakai soup
	U.S.A. # 14 - New England Clam Chowder
	Ghana # 24 - Nkrakra with Fufu Dumplings

Group - H Belgium # 11 - Waterzooi soup

      Russia # 22 - Golden Beet Borscht

      Algeria # 27 - Algerian Shorba soup

      Korean Republic #53- Spicy Jjamppong soup

Group A

Brazil # 10 - Black Bean and Chicken Soup

Croatia # 16 - Northern Croatian Black Bean Soup

Mexico # 21 - Albondigas Soup

Cameroon #50 - Groundnut (Peanut) and Chicken Soup

BRALIZ  **RANKED # 10**

Black bean and Chicken Soup

INGREDIENTS:

- 2 oz / 60 ml Olive oil
- 1 med white onion - small diced
- 3 stalks celery - small diced
- 1 med carrot - small diced
- 1 tbsp / 15 ml crushed garlic
- 3 chicken thighs, vegetable trim and 2 liters of water / 64 oz
- 4 oz / 120 grams Black Beans (soaked overnight or cooked before hand)
- 1 cup / 250 ml - mango nectar
- 4 oz / 125 ml - crushed tomatoes
- 4 oz / 125 ml- cider vinegar
- ½ bunch fresh cilantro-chopped fine.

SEASONINGS: Cumin, crushed chillies, thyme, salt & pepper to taste.

METHOD:

Saute onions, carrots and celery in olive oil, then add the garlic. You will notice that I never saute garlic with the vegetables, but that I add the garlic after the vegetables have been sautéed.The garlic becomes very bitter if scorched or burnt. Add the stock and mango nectar and crushed tomatoes & cooked black beans and simmer for about 30 minutes. Add vinegar and season to taste with salt & pepper, crushed chillies and cumin and thyme. Add cooked chicken and finish with chopped cilantro. I realize as I get further into the book, these soups are really so unique unto themselves,and it has been a joy to have tasted all of them.

CROATIA ■ ■ RANKED # 16

Northern Croatian Black Bean Soup

I used 3 types of beans in this recipe. Garbanzo - also known as chick peas, navy beans and kidney beans. Soaking the beans or even cooking them ahead of time will save you a boatload of time.

INGREDIENTS:

- 4 oz / 112 grams of each of the different beans
- 2 oz oil / 60 ml olive oil or vegetable oil.
- 1.5 medium onion - small dice
- 1 carrot - small dice
- 2 stalks of celery - small dice
- 2 medium sized tomatoes
- 6 oz of pork sausage - Pre cooked and cooled cut into small pieces.This will be added at a later time.
- 2 liters / 8 cups of vegetable stock
- 1 tbsp / 15 ml of crushed garlic

SEASONINGS: salt, pepper, thyme, paprika, chillies and basil.

METHOD:

Like I mentioned at the top of the page, soak the beans overnight or cook them ahead of time. Saute the vegetables until the onions are clear or translucent. Add the garlic and the stock and simmer for about 20 minutes. If you roast the tomatoes prior to using in the soup-this will change the flavour. The difference in taste is quite nice, compared to just adding to the soup. Add the sausage and simmer for about 30 minutes, add the beans, seasonings and salt and pepper to taste. The only way to avoid this soup from being overly salty is by adding all of the ingredients before finishing the seasonings.You can thicken with a slurry of cornstarch and cold water.(this is optional). By sticking to the traditional recipe of using the sausage this adds a dynamic flavour to the soup. Your seasonings if using the sausage will be changed according to taste. This is a very hearty soup, a meal in itself.

MEXICO ▌▌ ▌ RANKED # 21

Albondigas Soup

INGREDIENTS:

- 1.5 medium onions — sliced thin
- 1.5 carrots — sliced thin
- 2 stalks celery—sliced thin
- I tbsp / 15 ml crushed garlic
- 3 pieces of chicken thighs and legs
- 1.5 liters / 48 oz of water
- 4 oz / 100 ml crushed tomato
- 4 oz / 92 grams peas
- 1/2 bunch chopped cilantro
- 1/2 cup / 4 oz cooked rice

SEASONINGS: Oregano, crushed chillies, thyme, cilantro, fresh lime (both zeste and juice) of 1 lime. Salt and pepper to taste.

METHOD:

Saute the onions, celery and carrots once again until the onions become clear. Refrain from carmelizing the onions as this will colour the soup. Add the garlic sautéing gently. Then add the chicken stock and simmer. After simmering for about ¾ of an hour then add the cooked chicken, crushed tomatoes, cooked rice, peas and cilantro. Add the rest of the seasonings and finish the soup to your liking, add the chillies - but be careful. When I make soups I like to have them hearty and full flavoured with lots of vegetables and stuff. So when you eat a bowl you will have a hearty meal. Served with fresh bread etc... you won't need much more. You can thicken this soup with a slurry of cornstarch and cold water. But again that is optional.

CAMEROON ▮▮ RANKED # 50

Groundnut (Peanut) and Chicken Soup

INGREDIENTS:

- 3 oz / 100 ml vegetable oil
- 3 oz / 84 grams flour
- 1 tbsp / 15 ml crushed garlic
- 1 medium white onion - diced small
- 1 medium carrot - diced small
- 3 chicken legs and thighs *
- 2 liters / 8 cups water * Make a stock with the chicken,vegetable trim and water
- 2 fresh tomatoes - small dice
- 1 tbsp / 15 ml crushed garlic
- ½ green pepper - thin sliced
- ½ cup / 4 oz / 112 grams peanuts - roasted.
- Cilantro - 1/3 bunch chopped
- Chipotle pepper or ancho pepper- to taste
- 2 oz / 60 ml heavy cream - optional

SEASONINGS: Salt and pepper & thyme, chili powder, cumin and chillies to taste.

METHOD:

Saute onions and carrots, with a couple of ounces of vegetable oil, until the onions are translucent. Add the garlic and saute.Add the flour and stir until smooth. Make sure your stock is cold - once again to prevent a lumpy soup. Gently simmer for about ½ hour, then add the fresh tomatoes and the cooked chicken and season to taste.Finish with the heavy cream for texture. Add the chopped cilantro and chopped peanuts. Season to taste and then add the finely sliced or slivered green peppers as a garnish. When working with fresh herbs always add at the end. When working with dry herbs add about ½ way through the cooking procedure as they take more time to affect the flavour as compared to fresh herbs.

Group B

Spain # 1 - Caldo Gallego

Netherlands # 9 - Dutch Potato and Bacon soup

Chile # 15 - Spicy Seafood soup

Australia # 56 - Australian Pumpkin soup

SPAIN  RANKED # 1

Caldo Gallego

INGREDIENTS :

- 8 oz / 750 grams Navy Beans - Soaked overnight in 1 liter / 32 of water.
- 2 oz / 65 mls vegetable oil.
- 2 medium onions - thin sliced
- 1 carrot - thin sliced
- 3 stalks of celery - thin sliced
- 10 ml chopped fresh garlic
- 1 ham bone and 2 liters of cold water(save all the vegetable trim) for making the stock
- 4 oz / 125 grams of cured ham- thin sliced / chorizo or merguez sausage.
- 2 medium potato - peeled and cut into ½ inch pieces and cooked ½ way. Saving the stock from the potatoes.
- ½ bunch of leafy greens - such as turnip greens / kale / swiss chard etc.
- ⅓ bunch of fresh parsley.

SEASONINGS: Thyme, chillies, basil, salt and coarse black pepper to taste.

METHOD:

Soak the beans overnight in cold water. Cook the beans separately, until soft not mushy. Saute the vegetables in the oil, until the onions turn a clear or transluscent colour - not brown. Add the chopped fresh garlic. This is when you would add the Ham stock - which was made earlier with the ham bone, 2 liters water and all the vegetable trim. Please familiarize yourself with the chapter on making stocks. Cook the sausage before hand. This will prevent the amount of extra fat from getting into the soup, and this also prevents the soup from becoming cloudy. So to get back to making the soup, after you have added the garlic , add the stock and then simmer for 30 - 40 minutes at a moderate heat. Add the ½ cooked potatoes and thin sliced ham or chorizo and the beans. Let simmer for about 15 - 20 more minutes so the flavour from the ham / sausage leeches into the soup. Season to taste and then add the leafy greens cut into what is known as chiffonade. Thin sliced greens. This is used as a garnish. Then add the parsley chopped and voila. Just to think only 24 more soups. - Good luck ….

NETHERLANDS ▮ ▮ RANKED # 9

Dutch Potato and Bacon Soup

INGREDIENTS:

- 4 oz / 100 ml butter
- 4 oz / 92 grams of flour
- 2 tsp / 10 ml crushed garlic
- 8 oz / 225 grams of bacon - pre cook the bacon and chop into small pieces.
- 1 medium onions - thin sliced
- 1.5 liters / 48 oz of vegetable stock
- 3 medium potatoes - cut into ½ inch pieces and pre cooked.(once again save the potato stock)
- 4 oz / 100 ml heavy cream.
- 3- 4 oz / 84 grams - 112 grams mature Dutch cheese.
- a few fresh chives, and some fresh rosemary.

SEASONINGS: Thyme, chillies, tarragon salt and white pepper to taste.

METHOD:

Saute the onions in the butter until clear. Add the garlic and saute a bit more. Add the flour mixing slowly until your roux (equal amounts of fat/butter and flour. A method used to thicken soups is sort of dry using a wooden spoon. Slowly add the vegetable stock stirring with a whisk. Simmer for 15 minutes then add the ½ cooked potatoes. Cook for a few minutes more and add the bacon. Cook at a simmer for another 10 minutes and then add the cheese (grated) into the soup. Do not cook hard as the soup can break if too hot. Add the rosemary - not to much,season to taste and finish with heavy cream for texture. If the soup is too thick add the potato stock until you have your desired thickness.

CHILE ▮ ▮ RANKED # 15

Spicy Seafood Soup

INGREDIENTS:

- 3 oz / 100 ml olive oil
- 1.5 medium onions - sliced thin
- 1 medium carrots - sliced thin
- 2 stalks of celery - sliced thin
- ½ bunch of leeks - sliced and washed (use mainly the whites)
- 1 tbsp / 15 ml crushed garlic
- 1x 28 oz can of clams - (save the juice)
- 4 oz / 92 grams of shrimp meat
- 6oz / 168 grams mussels
- 6oz / 200 ml crushed tomatoes
- ½ red pepper - sliced thin
- ½ green pepper - sliced thin
- 2 medium potatoes - peeled and diced 1 inch pieces cooked ½ way (save the stock)
- 1 litre / 32 oz of vegetable stock
- ⅓ bunch of cilantro chopped

SEASONINGS: Thyme,basil,paprika,chili powder, fresh cilantro and salt and pepper to taste.

METHOD:

Saute the onions, carrots and celery in vegetable or olive oil until the onions are translucent. Add the garlic and gently saute. Add the vegetable stock and potato stock and crushed tomatoes simmer for about 30 minutes then add the partially cooked potatoes and juice from the clams. When using canned clams and baby shrimp always add to the soup near the end as they are already cooked and will get chewy if cooked too long. Add the herbs, spices and seasonings and adjust the taste to your liking. At the last minute turn up the heat and add the fresh mussels and cover the pot - this will cook the mussels quicker and keep the flavour in the broth then you can now add the shrimp and clams. A fresh baguette with this is the perfect touch.

AUSTRALIA ⬛ RANKED # 56

Australian Pumpkin Soup

Pumpkins and other squash make for excellent soups, which are in my opinion highly underrated! So some day the squash will get the recognition they rightfully deserve.

INGREDIENTS:

- 2 medium onions- diced
- 4 oz / 100 ml butter
- 4 oz / 168 grams of flour
- 2 tsp / 10 ml crushed garlic
- ½ medium pumpkin - depending on the size. (cleaned, peeled and roasted)
- 2 liters / 64 oz water
- 3 chicken thighs and legs
- 4 oz / 100 ml of heavy cream
- 4 oz / 168 grams of cooked black beans
- Creme fraiche - (garnish)
- Cilantro (optional)

SEASONINGS: Thyme, basil, chillies, salt and pepper to taste.

METHOD:

Roast the pumpkin in the oven for about 30 minutes, and when the pumpkin is light brown in colour then add to the pot sauteing the onions in butter until they become clear, then add the garlic, and then add the flour, making sure that the roux (combination of butter and flour) does not colour. Add the cool stock slowly while whisking gently. Add the roasted pumpkin and simmer. Cook for about 30 minutes on slow heat. Strain and puree. Finish by adding the chicken, seasonings and heavy cream for texture and then when serving, add a small spoon of black bean and a squirt of creme fraiche to finish. I like this soup with a touch of ancho pepper or even a little chipotle pepper. Like I mentioned earlier Cilantro is optional. But boy does it ever add a nice touch. The heavy cream is used to give the soup a richness of flavour and texture. This is the first mention of creme Fraiche in the book. Here is a very simple/ but not a traditional recipe. 50ml/2 oz sour cream, 50ml/2 oz whipping cream and a dash of lemon juice.

Group C

Colombia # 4 - Chicken and Potato soup

Greece # 12 - Mavromatika Fasolia me Loukanko

Cote d'Ivoire # 17 - Yam and Chicken soup

Japan # 48 - Red Miso and Pork soup

COLOMBIA ██ RANKED #4

Chicken and Potato Soup

INGREDIENTS :

- 3 oz /90 ml olive oil
- 1.5 medium onions - small dice
- 2 small carrots - small dice
- 3 stalks of celery - small dice
- 1 tbsp /15 ml chopped fresh garlic
- 2 liters of water
- 3 chicken thighs and legs
- 2 small potatoes - Russets (peeled and cut into 1 inch pieces and cooked ½ way) - save the potato stock.
- ⅓ bunch fresh cilantro
- 4 oz / 120 grams small pasta -already cooked
- zeste and juice from 1 fresh lemon - If you don't have a zester use a peeler and peel the lemon and chop the the skin fine.
- Capers and Avocado - sliced the avocado thin as a garnish not the capers. By the way capers are cool.

SEASONINGS: Cumin, Saffron, chili powder, salt and pepper to taste.

METHOD :

Make the chicken stock with the water, all the vegetable trim and a bay leaf. Simmer for 1 hour or there abouts. Saute the vegetables in the oil and when the onions are clear add the garlic and then add the chicken stock. Simmer for about 30 minutes - then add the saffron, chicken meat removed from the bones, the ½ cooked potatoes and pasta. Season to taste - but remember that Saffron is very unique in flavour and too much can be overpowering. So do be careful with the Saffron. Add the potato stock and the cilantro chopped and the avocado and capers as a garnish. Another garnish for this soup is a salsa.

GREECE ▮ RANKED # 12

Mavromatika Fasolia me Loukanko

I was somewhat curious about this soup, as with most exposure to Greek soups has been nothing out of the ordinary. Well how wrong was I. This is a very traditional soup but I found it quite refreshing to say the least.

INGREDIENTS:

- 2 onions - thin slice
- 1 medium carrot - thin slice
- 3 stalks of celery - thin slice
- 6 oz / 168 grams of sausage - Andouille or chorizo or Merguez - Cooked and diced small.
- 2 tsp / 10 ml crushed garlic
- 2 leaves of chard - thin sliced or (chiffonade) - Thick stock removed.
- 64 oz / 2 liters of vegetable stock
- 4 oz / 92 grams of white bean (precooked)
- 2 lemons — zested and juice from the same lemons. If you do not have a zester,peel the lemon and chop the peel.

SEASONINGS: salt, pepper, thyme, oregano and chillies.

METHOD:

Saute the onions, carrots and celery in olive oil. Add garlic and sauté a bit more. If you cook the beans ahead of time it saves a lot of time. Add the stock and gently simmer. Pre cook the sausage separately so as to cut down on the amount of fat that goes into the soup.This also prevents the soup from becoming cloudy.

Add the beans and the sausage - (cut into 1/2 inch pieces).

Let simmer gently for about 1/2 an hour. Now season according to your taste. Before you complete the final seasonings - add zeste from the lemon and then squeeze the juice from the same lemons. Avoid getting seeds in the soup. The zeste adds a totally new dimension to the soup. I have found that by adding a slurry of cornstarch to the soup prevents the soup from being too runny. The lemon really adds to the uniqueness of the soup.

COTE D'IVOIRE ■ ■ RANKED # 17

Yam and Chicken Soup

As you hopefully make your way through this book of World Cup soups you will notice that the key to a good soup is a simple stock, made usually from the trim of the vegetables and cold water. Some soups will call for a chicken stock or pork or fish. With this soup the stock will be made from chicken. Use the same procedure as the vegetable stock but use the thighs of the chicken and the vegetable trim. The difference between these stocks is the cooking time. A vegetable stock will be ready after about 30 minutes of simmering, whereas a chicken stock will take approximately 1.5 hours.

INGREDIENTS:

- 2 medium onions - peeled and diced fine
- 2 carrots- peeled and diced fine
- 2 oz / 56 grams of fresh garlic
- ⅓ bunch fresh cilantro - chopped fine
- 3 medium yams - peeled and diced into 1 inch pieces
- 3 chicken thighs and 2 liters / 64 oz water and your vegetable trim. Made ahead of time
- 3 oz / 84 grams butter
- 3 oz / 84 grams flour.

SEASONINGS: thyme, basil, cumin, coriander, salt and pepper and chillies to taste.

METHOD:

Saute the onions & carrots in butter until the onions become clear, add garlic and cook for another minute. Add flour and then add chicken stock and diced yams. You don't have to worry so much about the rule of thumb pertaining to cold stock, warm roux with this soup as you will puree the finished product. Simmer for about 1 hour at a low to medium heat. Puree the mixture and then add the cooked chicken. Season to taste with salt and pepper, thyme and crushed chillies. You may add curry or cumin to this soup as it will change the dynamics of the soup. Finish with a small amount of chopped cilantro for taste.

JAPAN ▮ RANKED # 48

Red Miso and Pork Soup

This is one of the simplest soups I've ever made - but despite being so simple it remains a savoury and rewarding treat.

INGREDIENTS:

- 8 oz / 225 ml package red miso paste
- vegetable stock to taste - use only what you want as the miso carries the flavour for this soup
- 4 oz / 92 grams of pulled pork
- 2-3 oz / 60-90 ml of soya sauce
- 3 green onions - sliced on an angle for garnish.

METHOD:

Bring approximately 2 liters of water to a rolling boil. Add the miso paste and simmer. Add the pulled pork and soya to taste. Go easy on the soya until you have tasted the soup first. If you find the soup too salty add less soya or more water. If you so choose you can thicken a bit with a slurry of cornstarch and cold water. When you are ready to serve add the green onion as a garnish. Very simple and tasty. A good quality miso paste makes all the difference!

Considering that this was the easiest soup of them all, the flavour was outstanding, and the customers where I work absolutely loved it. If you so choose you can add Tofu, cut into small pieces and add to the soup.

Group D

Uruguay # 6 - Chupin de Pescado soup

Italy # 7 - A Wedding soup

England # 13 - Oxtail soup

Costa Rica # 32 - Black Bean and Pork soup

URUGUAY  RANKED # 6

Chupin de Pescado Soup

INGREDIENTS:

- 1.5 medium onions - diced
- 1 medium carrot - diced
- 3 stalks of celery - diced
- 1/2 red pepper - sliced thin
- 1/2 green pepper - sliced thin
- 4 oz / 128 ml of crushed tomatoes
- 2oz / 56 grams teaspoon crushed garlic.
- 48 0z / 1.5 liters of vegetable stock
- 2 oz /68ml sherry

Mixed seafood — whatever you can find.Cod, prawns, shrimp meat etc. But definitely have a few mussels and clams for looks, as well as taste.The more seafood you have the better the flavour. 2 oz / 68 ml of sherry. The mussels and clams are cooked last.

SEASONINGS: thyme, basil, a pinch of allspice,tarragon,chillies, cilantro, salt and pepper to taste.

METHOD:

Saute the onions, carrots, and celery.Once again until the onions are clear not brown. I think that by now everyone should have the concept of sauteing vegetables down pat. Add garlic and sliced peppers. At this stage you will add your stock. You can use a vegetable stock here in this recipe because you will be simmering your assorted seafood just prior to serving so the seafood is cooked perfectly. Add the crushed tomatoes and vegetable stock and simmer gently. Add the sherry and season to taste, before you add the seafood.You do not want to overcook the seafood. Now just prior to serving add the seafood and simmer gently add the mussels and clams and cover for a few minutes. By covering the soup, the steam from the soup cooks the mussels and clams and the flavour goes back into the soup. The shrimp meat is already cooked so you can add them at the very end. The reason for me showing you a different method for doing a seafood soup is that by cooking fish directly in a soup, you can have a real cloudy product if you overcook the fish. If you have some salsa or cooked black beans lying about you can use either as a garnish.This was an outstanding soup.

ITALY  RANKED # 7

A Wedding Soup

This is called a wedding soup, but it is for a wedding of lots of vegetables and flavour, not a marriage. Reminder to save all the vegetable trim for your stock. Please note that when you make a stock you can always make it the day before.

INGREDIENTS:

- 1.5 medium onions – sliced thin
- 2-3 stalks of celery – sliced thin
- 1 medium carrot – peeled and sliced thin
- 4 oz / 120 grams of mushrooms – sliced thin
- 3 oz / 90 grams of orzo pasta
- 3 oz / 90 grams of peas
- 2 oz / 60 ml of olive oil
- ¼ bunch fresh parsley (chopped)
- Spinach-⅓ bunch - sliced thin or chiffonade - (stalks and stems removed)
- 1 oz / 30 grams fresh Garlic
- 2 liters / 64 oz of vegetable stock

SEASONINGS: thyme, oregano, basil, salt pepper and Chillies to taste.

Meatballs as a garnish, and grated Parmesan cheese.

METHOD:

Saute the onions, celery and carrots in the olive oil until the onions become clear or translucent -do not brown the vegetables. Add the mushrooms and garlic, sauté further and add the stock and simmer. Pre cook the orzo and cool off. Have the meatballs cooked and strained separately. Add the orzo and peas to the soup, as well as the chopped parsley and spinach, season to taste. Add the meatballs when serving the soup and sprinkle with grated Parmesan cheese. This soup could be vegan if you didn't add the meatballs. But then it wouldn't be "The Wedding Soup" would it?

MEATBALL RECIPE :

Is as follows-180 grams /6 oz of ground beef.chopped parsley, pinch of thyme 1 egg, 30 grams /1 oz bread crumbs, salt and pepper to taste. Add the egg, parsley, thyme and chillies and salt & pepper to the ground. Mix together and then roll into little meatballs. Adding the breadcrumbs will bind the meatballs so they don't fall apart.You may need to add a bit more bread crumb if you find that they (the meatballs) don't hold together. Pre cook the meatballs (the reason for pre cooking the meatballs ahead is the soup won't have any extra fat and your soup won't be cloudy) and strain. Set aside to be added to the soup when you are ready to serve. When you season the soup to your liking add the meatballs,cooked orzo and parmesan cheese as garnish.

ENGLAND ■ ■ RANKED # 13

Oxtail Soup

I wasn't sure as to what kind of soup I was going to do for Merry old England, well cause they (the English) are not really know for their culinary expertise but with some good chefs coming out of England things are looking up. They have made some leaps and bounds recently. I could have done a Mulligatawny or a Cock-a- leekie. This soup is rich in flavour and rich in tradition, but is a bit time consuming as you have to get some oxtail.Then you have to brown them, cook them and cool the stock. A very time consuming process. But boy it's woth it. Cool them, and clean the fat off them, and remove the meat from the bones and then make the soup.

INGREDIENTS:

- 2 lbs / 1 kg oxtails(lightly coated in flour and browned)
- 3 oz / 100ml vegetable oil. Use this oil to brown the oxtails.
- 3 oz / 100 ml vegetable oil.
- I med onion - diced
- 3 celery stalks - diced
- 2 carrots - peeled and diced
- 2 liters / 64 ounces of water and vegetable trim - to make the beef stock.
- 2 medium sized potato - diced and cooked 1/2 way. (saving the stock)

SEASONINGS: Salt & pepper, thyme and oregano

METHOD :

Coat the oxtails in flour and slowly brown in the oven for about ½ an hour, then place in 2 liters cold water and with all the vegetable trimmings. Make a stock by slowly simmering adding the vegetable trim from onions,celery and carrots to the stock as well as a bay leaf, whole black peppercorns and a dash of salt. Cook for about an hour and a bit. Remove the oxtails and let cool. When the tails are cool,remove the fat and the meat from the tails - discard the fat and save the meat. Strain and cool the stock and skim the fat from the stock.The next procedure is saute' the diced vegetables in the oil and pre cook the potatoes until ½ done once again saving the stock.

Add the beef stock to the sautéed vegetables and also some of the potato stock and simmer. Add the meat and season to taste. Remember that the potatoes are optional, and also pot barley has also been used in this recipe. This is an old traditional meal that fed families for a couple of days at a minimal cost.- The real kicker for this soup is a rich tasty stock.

COSTA RICA ▉ ▉ RANKED # 32

Black Bean and Pork Soup

Wow - Black beans,Navy Beans- well any bean or lentils are great.You can do so much with them.They are healthy, and flavourful as well. You can make most of the soups in this book vegetarian by replacing the meat stock with a vegetable stock - and of course withholding the meat itself. A black bean soup like this is just as tasty without the meat. But, it's all on how you season your soup. Lotsa veggies, etc.

INGREDIENTS:

- 2 small onions - diced
- 2 celery stalks - diced
- 1 medium carrot - diced
- 2 cups / 500 ml of dry black beans - soaked overnight or if you want,cook them the day before with lots of water until they are soft,not mushy.By soaking before hand is supposed to cut down on your bodies reaction to using beans in a diet. Need I say more.
- 1.5 Liters / 48 oz vegetable stock
- 6oz / 168 grams of cheap cuts of pork - cheaper, tougher, cuts often yield better flavours to the soup - I use pulled pork. Please note if using a tough cut you will have to cook for about the same length of time as a beef stock. With pulled pork the flavour is great and no cooking time.

Serrano peppers - these are very hot so be careful not to use too many, and to wash your hands after using or handling them.

SEASONINGS: Cilantro, thyme, basil, salt and pepper to taste.

I like to garnish this soup with fresh salsa and a dollop of sour cream - the contrast in colours is spectacular - rich black, bright red and brilliant white.

METHOD:

Saute diced vegetables in olive oil until translucent. Use the vegetable trimmings and pork to make a stock, but don't bring it to a hard boil as this can render out fats making the stock cloudy. Cook your black beans while you are preparing your vegetables or like I mentioned at the beginning of this recipe. Add the stock and beans to the soup simmer for about 15-20 minutes then add the pork and the other seasonings to taste. Then carefully add the Serrano peppers-finely diced,with the seeds removed.Remember that the pith or white insides of peppers and the seeds are the spicy parts. The key to this and many soups is how you season it.Garnish with fresh salsa and sour cream just before serving.

Group E

Switzerland # 8 - Potato and Bacon soup

France # 20 - Pumpkin, Black Bean and Ham soup

Ecuador # 23 - Summer Squash soup

Honduras # 43 - Sopa de Caracol soup

SWITZERLAND ▮ RANKED # 8

Potato and Bacon Soup

INGREDIENTS:

- 8 Rashers or slices of bacon.
- 1.5 medium onions - small dice.
- 2 stalks of celery - small dice.
- 1 medium carrot - peeled and small dice.
- 2 medium russet potatoes - peeled and diced into 1 inch pieces. Cooked 1/2 way. Save the potato stock for adding to the soup.
- 3 oz / 100 ml vegetable oil
- 3 oz / 84 grams of flour
- 1.5 liters of vegetable stock
- 2 tsp / 10 ml crushed garlic.
- 3 oz / 84 grams of Swiss cheese
- 3 oz / 100 ml of Heavy cream.(whipping cream)

This may seem like an awful lot of ingredients but it's not.

SEASONINGS: Thyme, Basil, Oregano and salt and White pepper to taste.

METHOD :

Saute the sliced bacon first for a few minutes or until the bacon is about ½ cooked.Then add the onions, celery and carrots with the vegetable oil. When the bacon is becoming crispy and the onions clear, then add the crushed garlic. Add the flour gradually until the oil and bacon fats are relatively dry. Slowly add the vegetable stock (make sure the stock is cold).This prevents lumps in your soup. Simmer gently for about 30 minutes and then add the potato stock only as needed, after the soup has cooked out.You will then have an idea as to how thick you want your soup. By saving some of the potato stock you get the desired thickness you want.

Add the heavy cream, Swiss cheese and simmer for about 5 minutes or so and then season to taste. If you season the soup before the cream and cheese have fully cooked you can end up having a very salty soup cause of the cheese and bacon. Also be careful you don't cook this soup hard as the cheese can end up curdling.

FRANCE ■ ▊ RANKED # 20

Pumpkin, Black Bean and Ham Soup

INGREDIENTS:

- 4 oz / 92 grams of butter
- 4 oz / 92 grams of flour
- 1 medium white onion - diced
- 1 x carrot - diced
- 15 ml crushed fresh garlic
- 1 medium pumpkin-peeled and seeds removed. Dice into small pieces. Approximately ½ pieces.
- 6 oz / 168 grams of black beans-you can cook these overnight or before hand.
- 6 oz / 168 grams of ham. Any kind of ham is fine.Black Forest,Gammon etc..small dice.
- 1 cup / 240 ml crushed tomatoes
- 1.5 liters / 6 cups of vegetable stock - (made from the trim of the onions, carrots and celery)
- 3 oz / 100 ml of heavy cream
- Vinegar to taste
- 1 cup / 240 ml of corn
- ⅓ bunch of parsley - washed and chopped fine - this is used as a garnish.

SEASONINGS: Thyme,tarragon, chillies,some basil salt and white pepper to taste.

METHOD:

You can roast the cut up pumpkin in the oven as this changes the dynamics of the soup. Saute diced onions and carrots in butter until the onions become translucent, then stir in the flour to create a relatively dry roux. Slowly add vegetable stock to the roux while stirring with a whisk. Add the roasted pumpkin and bring the soup to a simmer at a medium heat for roughly 20 - 25 minutes. Then puree in a food processor or blender. Add the ham, corn, crushed tomato, and cook for about 10 minutes. Then add the beans and cook for 15-20 minutes stirring occasionally.

Add the herbs and seasonings for taste. Finish with heavy cream for texture, and garnish with creme fraiche and chopped parsley. Voila.

A SOUP FROM FRANCE:

Wow! Choosing this soup was as difficult as choosing the soup for England, but for totally different reasons - the French sure can cook, whereas the English and no disrespect to the English, but they are not in the same league as the French when it comes to cooking.

ECUADOR  **RANKED # 23**

Summer Squash Soup

INGREDIENTS:

- 1 x good sized butternut squash. Peeled and cubed small dice.
- 3 oz / 100ml olive oil
- 1 medium onion - small dice
- 2 stalks of celery - small dice
- 1/2 carrot - small dice
- 1.5 liters / 48 oz - vegetable stock
- 2 tsp / 10 ml crushed garlic
- 2 fresh tomatoes - diced and roasted.
- 1/2 red pepper - thin slice
- 1/2 green pepper - thin sliced
- 3 oz / 100 ml butter
- 3 oz / 84 grams flour - This makes a roux
- 1/4 bunch fresh cilantro - chopped fine

SEASONINGS: Thyme,white pepper, tarragon,salt and Aji Amarillo paste.

METHOD:

In a pan with the olive oil roast the squash in the oven till the squash is carmelized or a nice golden color. You can roast the tomatoes at this time with the squash. Saute the onions, celery and carrots in the butter,when the onions are translucent add the garlic and cook for another minute. Add the flour till the butter is soaked up and the roux is dry, not bone dry. Add the vegetable stock and cook for about 20 minutes at a low heat.This cooks the flour and then you can correct the thickness. Add the squash and tomato to the soup. Puree this mixture and then add on the assorted peppers, thinly sliced and fresh chopped cilantro.

Adjust the seasonings, but the key here is add the Aji Amarillo paste accordingly - but do be careful as this is quite spicy. If the soup is too thick add some more stock until you have the thickness of the soup that is to your liking. If you want - you can add some heavy cream to get that smoothness.This is optional.

HONDURAS ▮ RANKED # 43

Sopa de Caracol Soup

This soup is definitely in my top ten!

INGREDIENTS:

- 2 oz / 60 ml vegetable oil
- 1 medium onion - thinly sliced
- 1 carrots - thinly sliced3
- 2 stalks celery - thinly sliced
- 1 tbsp / 15 ml chopped garlic
- 1 small tin - coconut milk
- 1.5 liters of vegetable stock
- Conch (I used 1 x 14 ounce can of baby clams, as conch is hard to come by in Canada - strain and save the juice). If you have access to fresh conch all the better.
- 1 tbsp / 15 ml fresh ginger (peeled and chopped fine)
- ½ bunch chopped cilantro
- Zeste and juice from 1 fresh lime
- Assorted fresh seafood - cod or scallops, throw in some prawns and don't forget mussels in the shell. Approximately 2-3 oz of each, about 2 or 3 mussels per bowl.

SEASONINGS: Basil, thyme, chillies, salt and pepper to taste.

NOTE: that if you want you can add some rice to the soup. But that is optional.

METHOD:

Saute the onions, celery and carrots once again until the onions become clear. Refrain from caramelizing the onions as this will colour the soup. Add the garlic and ginger sautéing gently. Then add the coconut milk, vegetable stock and clam juice. Simmering gently.

Now the key to making any kind of seafood soup is to do your utmost not to overcook the seafood, so to make this work, finish seasoning the soup with lime juice and zeste, cilantro and other seasonings. Then add the canned clams, or conch, your assorted seafood and gently simmer. The last step is add the mussels and cover for about 1 minute - just long enough to bring them to the temperature of the soup. Voila… The reason for covering the soup when you add the mussels is the juice or flavour from the mussels goes back into the soup adding even more flavour. This soup is great the same day, but is not a great reheat.

Group F

Argentina # 3 - Locro de Argentine / Navy Bean and Corn soup

Bosnia and Herzegovina # 19 - Chicken, bacon and Okra soup

Iran # 34 - Asheh Reshteh soup

Nigeria # 41 - Okra, Chicken and Uziza Leaf soup

ARGENTINA ▌▐ RANKED # 3

Locro de Argentine / Navy Bean and Corn Soup

INGREDIENTS :

- 3 oz / 90 ml vegetable oil
- 2 small onions - thin slice
- 2 small carrots - thin slice
- 3 stalks of celery - thin slice
- 1 lb / 454 grams of beef short ribs
- 2 liters of water.
- 8 oz / 225 grams Navy beans - once again pre cooked / or soaked overnight.
- 4 oz / 115 grams corn niblets.
- 4 oz / 115 grams chorizo sausage.
- 1 tbsp / 15 ml crushed fresh garlic.

SEASONINGS: Chili powder,Paprika, Basil, Thyme, Salt & Pepper to taste. I add a few crushed chillies for a little bit more oomph.This is purely up to you. But this soup can handle a little more punch.

METHOD :

Saute the vegetables except the garlic in the vegetable oil, once again until the onions are clear. Make the stock with the short ribs and vegetable trim. Add the garlic and the beef stock and simmer for 30 minutes or there abouts. Pre cook the chorizo and slice thinly. When the stock is finished, strain and remove the meat from the beef ribs. Add the cooked chorizo, navy beans, corn and beef. Season to taste - remembering that the chorizo is spicy and watch your salt in this soup, again because of the sausage. Finish seasoning to your taste. This is a hearty soup full of flavour.

BOSNIA AND HERZEGOVINA ■ ▨ RANKED # 19

Chicken, Bacon and Okra Soup

INGREDIENTS:

- 3 chicken thighs and legs
- 64 oz / 2 liters of water
- 4 oz / 92 grams of fresh okra
- 4 oz / 92 grams of bacon or cured ham - bacon is my favorite for this recipe.
- 4 oz cooked rice
- 2 medium onions - thin slice
- 1 med carrot - thin slice
- 2 stalks celery - thin slice
- 2 oz / 50 ml of vegetable oil
- 2 tsp / 10 ml crushed garlic
- 4 oz / 100 ml- crushed tomatoes
- 2oz / 50 ml Lemon juice

SEASONINGS: Crushed chillies, thyme, oregano, basil, ancho peppers, paprika, chopped fresh parsley salt and white pepper to taste.

METHOD :

First thing to do is make the stock with cold water, chicken thighs and vegetable trim. Pre cook the bacon - this prevents the soup from becoming greasy or fatty. Mind you, you can saute the vegetables in the bacon, but that can be tricky as the bacon takes longer to cook than vegetables,so your vegetables can become too brown before the bacon is cooked. Cook the chicken and vegetable trim for about 1 hour-gently not a hard boil as this will give you a greasy and cloudy stock. Strain and use the chicken stock for the soup and finish with the lemon juice.

Saute thinly sliced onions, celery, and carrots and the very unique food —OKRA - in the oil.Once again until the onions are clear, not brown. Add garlic and the stock and the crushed tomatoes and the cooked chicken diced small. Now you can simmer for about 1/2 an hour.This soup can handle a little spice, so be brave, not foolish. If you find these soups too thin you can add cornstarch and cold water to get the acquired thickness this way. Finish seasoning with the herbs and spices, a dash of lemon juice and sour cream as a garnish.Once again the way one uses the seasonings makes the difference. Please note that Okra when cooked goes slimey and is quite bland in flavour - so you can certainly do things with this member of the Tuber family. Okra can be used as a thickening agent in some soups. So adjust the seasonings and enjoy.

IRAN  **RANKED # 34**

Asheh Reshteh Soup

I made a slight change in this recipe for I could not find the right persian noodle (Reshteh)

INGREDIENTS:

- 3 oz / 100 ml olive oil
- 1 large onion - thinly sliced
- 3 chicken thighs and legs and 2 liters of water for the stock.
- 3 types of beans - kidney, chickpeas and lentils.
- 1 red onion - thin sliced and cooked crispy -to be used as a garnish at the end.
- 1/3 bunch cilantro
- ¼ bunch mint
- handful of spinach - thinly sliced (chiffonade)
- pinch of saffron
- 4 oz / 100 ml cooked reshteh - this type of noodle may be difficult to get, but try your darndest / hardest to find it.
- 2 tsp / 10 ml crushed garlic
- 1 /2 a bunch of fresh mint and parsley - chopped for garnish

SEASONINGS: turmeric, thyme coriander and chillies,salt and peppers to taste.

Note of reference pertaining to the beans. Raw chickpeas or garbanzo beans take a fair amount of time to cook, so I use canned chick peas. I also use canned kidney beans as well. But do cook your lentils in the soup. Use about 4 oz /12 grams approximately.

METHOD:

Sauté the onions in the oil then add the garlic and sauté for a little bit more. Saute the turmeric, coriander and saffron. Strain the chicken stock and clean the chicken off the bones. Dice the chicken into small pieces and lentils and simmer slowly. Add the chicken and precooked beans and cook for another 20 minutes. Season to taste. The noodles are used as a garnish, then top with the crispy fried red onions. Note that the complexities of the seasonings in this soup are what makes it so unique in taste. Saffron, dill, turmeric and coriander. Remember - when using fresh herbs such as cilantro,parsley and the mint as well as the spinach it's best to add them all at the end - this keeps the flavours and textures intact, and makes them much more pronounced. This was real feast of flavours.

NIGERIA ▌▌ RANKED # 41

Okra, Chicken and Uziza Leaf Soup

INGREDIENTS:

- 3 oz / 100mls olive oil
- 1.5 medium onions - thinly sliced
- 1 carrot - thinly sliced
- 2 stalks of celery - thinly sliced
- 6 oz / 168 grams of fresh okra - sliced
- 2 plantain - When ready to add to the soup,cut off the ends, and cut lengthwise, and then cut into small diced pieces.
- 3 chicken legs and thighs -To make the stock.
- 1.5 liters / 48 oz chicken stock.
- 4 oz / 100 ml of pepper greens or Uziza - thin slice or chiffonade
- 2 tsp / 10 ml fresh crushed garlic

NOTE : 3

SEASONINGS: salt,pepper to taste,thyme,basil,tarragon and chillies - (careful) with the chillies for the Uziza sure kicks it up a bit. So when it comes to the final seasonings do be careful with the spice. Also since I am from Canada,we don't have a lot of exposure to something such as Uziza or plantains for that matter. So when I did this soup I added the Plantains with the peel still on, but the ends trimmed off. I found the flavour quite interesting to say the least.

METHOD:

Saute the vegetables in oil until the onions are clear, add the garlic, okra and plantain. Saute a bit more and add the chicken stock. Simmer for 30 minutes and add the chicken (cut into small pieces) simmer a bit more. Saute the pepper leaves and add to the soup.

Remember that the pepper leaves are quite spicy, so finish seasoning the soup after you have added the leaves. If desired, you can thicken with a slurry of cornstarch and cold water.

The ingredients of this soup have subtle flavours and rely on the pepper leaves to form the body of the flavour.

Group G

Germany # 2 - Graupensuppe / German Barley soup

Portugal # 5 - Kahakai soup

U.S.A. # 14 - New England Clam Chowder

Ghana # 24 - Nkrakra with Fufu Dumplings

GERMANY ▮▯ RANKED # 2

Graupensuppe / German Barley Soup

INGREDIENTS :

- 3 oz / 90 ml vegetable oil
- 1.5 medium onion - small dice
- 8 oz / 225 grams sliced fresh mushrooms
- 1 med carrot - small dice
- 2 stalks of celery - small dice
- 1 tbsp / 15 ml crushed garlic
- 1 lb beef short ribs / 454 grams - If you brown the ribs and roast in the oven this will create a beautiful, rich beef stock.
- 2. 5 liters / 5 cups of cold water
- 6 oz / 200 grams bacon - cook separately and pat to get excess grease off the bacon.
- 6 oz / 200 grams pot barley. (cook before hand) This will prevent the soup from becoming cloudy and this way you only add what you need for the soup. Some people like a thick soup, others don't.
- ⅓ bunch chopped parsley.

SEASONINGS: Thyme,Paprika, cracked chillies (to taste)salt and black pepper.

METHOD:

With this soup and other soups that call for bacon in it, I personally cook the bacon ahead of time, whereas traditional recipes saute the vegetables in the bacon to get a richer flavour. I saute the vegetables in vegetable oil until the onions are clear, then add the garlic and the beef stock. Simmer for about ½ an hour to 45 minutes. Remove the meat from the bones,add the cooked barley, not all. If you need or want to add more then do so. Add the bacon and meat from the beef bones and let simmer for another 10 minutes. This lets the bacon flavour come through before you add the rest of the seasonings. Finish the rest of the seasoning to taste.

PORTUGAL ▌▌ RANKED # 5

Kahakai Soup

INGREDIENTS:

- 2 medium onions - thin slice
- 1 med carrot - thin slice
- 2 stalks celery - thin slice
- 2 oz / 60 ml of vegetable oil
- 2 medium russet potatoes - peeled and diced into ½ inch pieces and cooked1/2 way. Save the stock
- 2 tsp / 10 ml crushed fresh garlic
- 4 oz / 120 grams crushed tomatoes
- 4 oz / 120 grams of chorizo sausage. Precook and dice into small pieces.
- 1/2 red pepper and ½ green pepper - thin sliced
- 1.5 liters / 6 cups of vegetable stock
- 4 oz / 120 grams of pre cooked kidney beans or red beans.

SEASONINGS: Crushed chillies, thyme, oregano, basil, ancho peppers, paprika, chopped parsley, salt and white pepper to taste.

METHOD:

First thing to do is make the stock with cold water and vegetable trim. Pre cook the chorizo - this prevents the soup from being overly greasy or fatty. Also cook the kidney beans before hand until soft.Saute thinly sliced onions, celery, and carrots in the oil.Once again until the onions are clear, not brown. Add garlic and the stock and the crushed tomatoes. Now you can simmer for about 1/2 an hour.This soup can handle a little spice or oomph.The finishing touch is adding the cooked potatoes, red and green peppers,chorizo and beans. If you find these soups too thin you can add cornstarch and cold water- also known as a slurry. Finish seasoning with the herbs and spices.This is an extremely hearty soup that packs a wallop of flavours.

U.S.A. ▌▐ RANKED # 14

New England Clam Chowder

INGREDIENTS:

- 1x 28oz. can of baby clams (strained saving the juice)
- 4 oz / 100 ml of butter
- 4 oz / 92 grams of flour
- 3 medium russet potatoes - peeled and diced in ½ inch pieces. Cook ½ way and save the stock
- 1 medium white - onion diced small
- 3 stalks of celery - diced small
- 1 medium carrot - diced small
- 1 tbsp / 15 ml crushed garlic
- 48 oz / 1.5 liters of vegetable stock
- 4 oz / 100 ml heavy cream or whipping cream
- 4 oz / 92 grams of cooked bacon

SEASONINGS: tarragon, crushed chilies, thyme, basil, salt and white pepper to taste.

METHOD:

Saute onions, carrots and celery in butter then add the garlic and lightly saute a little longer being careful not to burn the garlic. Slowly add the flour while stirring constantly and cook until mixture is relatively dry. Slowly add the clam juice and vegetable stock (once again making sure that your stock is cold so as to avoid lumps in the soup). After adding the stock simmer at a low temperature to cook out the taste of the flour. You can add some of the potato stock at this time in order to get the consistency you want. Add the clams, bacon, and cooked potatoes. Simmer for about 20 minutes and finish with heavy cream. Season with salt and pepper, tarragon and thyme and some cracked chillies for ooomph.

NOTE: In order to find out when potatoes are cooked ½ way, just remove one piece and try it.You want the potatoes still firm and not mushy, for you will eventually be adding the potatoes back into the soup, and will be cooking everything for a bit longer. After a while you will figure out the time involved in this procedure.

On a personal note this is one of my all time favourite soups.

GHANA  **RANKED # 24**

Nkrakra with Fufu Dumplings

INGREDIENTS:

- 4 oz / 100 ml vegetable oil
- 1.5 medium onions - diced
- 1 medium carrot - diced
- 4 oz / 92 grams mushrooms - thin sliced
- 1 red pepper - thin sliced.
- 1 lb / 454 grams of beef short bib - browned and used to make a rich beef stock.Use all the vegetable trim and 2 liters of cold water to make the stock. Strain after cooking for about an hour, saving the stock and removing the meat from the bones.
- 1 tbsp / 15 ml crushed garlic
- 4 oz / 100 ml of crushed tomatoes
- 1/3 of an eggplant - (thin slices lightly seasoned with salt) place on paper towel to soak up moisture that will be drawn out of the eggplant by the salt. This procedure will sort of prevent the eggplant from turning mushy - cut into small pieces.

SEASONINGS: thyme, basil, paprika, chillies,salt and pepper to taste.

METHOD:

Saute the onions and carrots in vegetable oil until the onions are translucent. Add the mushrooms and cook a bit more. Add the garlic and crushed tomatoes and beef stock. Add the beef and simmer gently for approximately 20 - 25 minutes. If you cooked the beef overnight this procedure cuts the cooking time in half. Add the seasonings and then pan fry the eggplant and red pepper and add to the soup last minute. Have the fufu dumplings made ahead of time and use as a garnish. Season the soup to taste.

RECIPE FOR FUFU DUMPLINGS:

- 1 cup potato flour
- 2 tsp baking powder
- ¼ tsp salt
- Dash of nutmeg
- ½ cup milk or water
- Chopped parsley (optional)

Have a bath of hot lightly salted water. Mix all the ingredients together the flour etc.. until the mixture is smooth. Don't overwork the mix. Get two spoons and shape the dumplings into well -small dumplings. Gently cook for about 2 minutes or until they are firm. You will want to make sure that they are fully cooked. They will firm up and not be mushy when they (the dumplings) are cooked. Uncooked dumplings can make your soup mushy and cloudy. Cool the dumplings in an ice bath and pat dry to stop the cooking process. You add the dumplings just prior to serving - but do make sure that the dumplings are hot and the soups is too.

Group H

Belgium # 11 - Waterzooi soup

Russia # 22 - Golden Beet Borscht

Algeria # 27 - Algerian Shorba soup

Korean Republic # 53 - Spicy Jjamppong soup

BELGIUM ▮▯ RANKED # 11

Waterzooi soup

Just a short note, as of completing this recipe I am now about 1/2 way through the book. And as to date this soup is probably the one I liked best. Throughout the book you will see these key words. - Chicken stock / Beef Stock etc. In order to have a good soup you need a good stock. Try to refrain from using powdered soup bases that are high in sodium. Check the make when you are forced to use a base. Mind you this book is geared towards the use of real stocks.

INGREDIENTS:

- 2 oz / 60 grams of butter
- 2 oz / 60 grams of flour
- 1.5 medium onions - diced
- 1 medium carrot - diced
- 3 stalks of celery - diced
- 2 tsp / 10 ml crushed garlic.
- 1 leek (all the white part of the leek and about 1/4 of the green part) - washed and sliced thin.
- 2 medium russet potatoes (peeled and diced in 1/2 inch pieces) - When cooking potatoes cover potatoes about 2 inches above the top of the potatoes. This allows for a better stock and also allows for evaporation. Cook ½ way and save the stock.
- 2 oz / 64 ml Vermouth
- 4 chicken thighs
- 2 liters / 64 oz of cold water and vegetable trim. Makes the stock
- 3 egg yolks and 2 oz of heavy cream.(mixed together) and kept separate for use in thickening this soup.

SEASONINGS: thyme,basil,tarragon,chillies and salt and pepper to taste.

METHOD:

Saute the onions, carrots,celery and leeks in butter until the onions are translucent or clear, add the garlic then add the flour and cook a bit more. Do not brown the roux. Add the chicken stock. Stirring gently with a whisk. At this point make sure that the stock is cold when the roux is hot. Gently cook so as not to burn, now add the stock from the potatoes. Add the Vermouth. Over the course of time the alcohol will cook off and the flavour will come out. Season with a little more tarragon than you would normally. Add the basil, thyme, chillies and white pepper and salt to taste. Now you will notice that in the ingredients you will see the egg yolks and heavy cream. In a separate bowl combine the egg yolks and cream together, whisk gently, do not make frothy.Take 2 large ladles of soup and add to the egg yolk mixture and when incorporated or mixed up completely add back to soup. Make sure that the soup is not boiling hard as this will scramble the yolks.There are a few recipes where you thicken soups this way.The egg yolks and cream add a very interesting taste and texture to this soup.

RUSSIA ■ RANKED # 22

Golden Beet Borscht

This is the real deal when it comes to eastern European soups and the types of soups that come from this area of the world. Harsh winters, short summers and a down to earth type of cooking. If you can't get golden beets then use regular beets.

INGREDIENTS:

- 1.5 lb / 750 grams of golden beets. Pre cook the beets until ½ cooked. Strain saving the beet stock. Cool off the beets so as to keep the beautiful rich colour of the beets. Save the beet greens.
- 3 oz / 100 ml vegetable oil
- 2 med white onion - diced
- 2 carrots peeled and diced
- 1 tbsp / 15 ml fresh garlic
- 6 oz / 168 grams - sliced green cabbage
- 1.5 liters / 48 oz vegetable stock
- Remaining beet stock already saved.
- 2 oz / 68 ml vinegar or to taste - Add by taste. This depends how tart you want the soup.
- Beet greens - Chiffonade (thin sliced) and used as a garnish.

SEASONINGS: thyme,oregano, dill and salt and pepper to taste.

METHOD:

Saute diced vegetables in the vegetable oil until the onions turn a clear colour. Add the sliced cabbage and saute for a few more minutes. Add the vegetable stock, beet stock and simmer for about 30 minutes.Then add the diced the beets to the stock. Add the vinegar to taste. Again you don't have use all of the vinegar.This is purely an individual thing. Season to taste with dill, oregano,salt, pepper and thyme. You can save the beet greens and sauté them. Add right at the end after you have seasoned your soup.That is just another option. Remember that this soup historically would feed the family for a while. Great taste and is pretty darn healthy for you. You can make this soup vegetarian or you can add pork.

ALGERIA

RANKED # 27

Algerian Shorba soup

This soup was new to me not that long ago, and a bit of a surprise. The complexities of the seasonings and layers of flavour make it a real treat!

INGREDIENTS :

- 2 medium onions - thinly sliced
- 1 medium carrot - thinly sliced
- 2 stalks celery - thinly sliced
- 3 oz / 100 mls of peanut oil
- 2 tsp /10 ml crushed garlic
- 4 oz /100 mls crushed tomatoes
- 3 Chicken thighs and legs for the stock. Cook with 2 liters of cold water.
- 4 oz / 112 grams of rice uncooked rice.
- Zeste and juice from 1 lemon.
- ⅓ bunch of fresh parsley - washed and chopped.Use as a garnish.

SEASONINGS: Crushed chillies, thyme, tarragon, basil, ancho peppers, paprika, chopped parsley. Salt and white pepper to taste. Juice and zest from 2 lemons.

METHOD:

First make the stock with cold water, chicken thighs and vegetable trimmings. You can always make this the previous day and strain. Clean the meat off the thighs and save for the soup. Use the stock for the soup.

Saute thinly sliced onions, celery, and carrots in the peanut oil until the onions are clear, not brown. Add the garlic, chicken stock and the crushed tomatoes. Now you can add the uncooked rice and simmer for about ½ an hour. This soup can handle a little spice or oomph. The finishing touch is adding the zest and lemon juice. To prepare the zest use a zester, though if you don't have one, use a peeler as this works if you peel the lemon and chop fine. Now you can add the chicken and finish the seasonings. If you find this soup to thin you can slowly stir in a cornstarch slurry made with cold water until you get the desired thickness.

The lemon is an unexpected and refreshing touch to this soup.

KOREAN REPUBLIC ■ RANKED # 53

Spicy Jjamppong Soup

Of all the soups I've made, this one has the most unique gathering of ingredients!

INGREDIENTS:

- 1 medium onion - thinly sliced
- 1 medium carrot - thinly sliced
- 1 leek - cut lengthways to clean, and then sliced thin crosswise
- 3 oz / 100 ml Shiitake mushrooms
- a couple twists of kelp
- 4 oz / 168 grams of pulled pork
- 2 tsp / 10 ml of fresh ginger - Peeled and chopped fine.
- 1 Tbsp / 15 ml crushed garlic
- 6oz / 168 grams of sliced green cabbage
- 3 field mushrooms - thinly sliced
- 3 oz / 100 ml of sesame oil
- A mixture of seafood (best to use an assortment of fresh mussels, clams, prawns, scallops, and whitefish)
- 1.5 Liter / 48 oz vegetable stock
- Fish sauce - a couple of splashes

SEASONINGS: pepper, chillies and salt to taste.

METHOD: Saute the onions, carrots and leeks and both types of mushroom with the sesame oil. Add the cabbage and ginger and garlic after the other vegetables are cooked halfway, sauté a bit more. Add the vegetable stock and simmer for about 10 minutes. Add your mixed seafood and cover for about 5- 10 minutes.Then add your mussels and clams and cover. Covering retains more flavour in the soup. Add the kelp-sliced, chillies and finish the seasoning and the last step is the splash of fish sauce. The broth is very flavourful but be careful not to overcook the seafood.